Milly, Molly
W.W. Webby

"We may look different but we feel the same."

W.W. Webby lived in the orchard between two old peach trees. He had eight legs, as all spiders do, and he was the friendliest spider Milly and Molly had ever met.

"Why are you so friendly?" Milly asked him one day.
"Because," answered W.W. Webby, "I love everybody."

"Everybody in the whole wide world?" asked Molly.
"Everybody in the whole wide world," he said. "There is no room for bigotry and racism in a spider's web."

Milly and Molly had no idea what bigotry and racism looked like but they had another idea. "Could you build us a World Wide Web?" they asked.

W.W. Webby thought for a moment.
Then he said, "Yes, yes, I think I could."
"You really could?" Milly and Molly
were excited.
"I have friends in very high places," he said. "I'm
sure I could."

"Don't be surprised if I disappear for a few days," W.W. Webby advised. "I'll be back."

Milly and Molly waited...

and waited.

Then, one morning, there was their World Wide Web.

It stretched from one mountain to the next, right across the world.

Milly and Molly found W.W. Webby lying back in his web.

"Please read the notice before you climb the ladder," was all he could say.
W.W. Webby was exhausted.

Day after day, Milly and Molly made new friends with children from all over the world.

They looked for bigotry and racism but they couldn't find them anywhere.

One night, there was an almighty storm.
Milly and Molly could hear the whirr
of a million pairs of shoes.

They could hear the wind thrashing about in the trees. And they feared for W.W. Webby in his web between the two old peach trees.

"You don't need to worry about me," said W.W. Webby, when Milly and Molly found him. "I can build a new web in no time."

And he did.

"I don't need to worry about you," he said. "You've built your web of friends, worldwide. An almighty storm can't change that either."

"What about our shoes?" Milly and Molly asked. "We can't find them anywhere."

W.W. Webby thought deeply for a moment. "To walk in someone else's shoes, is to really understand them," he said wisely.

"That way you can stomp on bigotry and racism, forever."

Milly liked the feel of her new shoes.
So did Molly. They were thankful they couldn't find bigotry and racism among their new friends, because they didn't want to stomp on anyone.